J
613.69
ADA

Surviving a Flood

by Heather Adamson

amicus readers
2

amicus readers

Say hello to amicus readers.

You'll find our helpful dog, Amicus, chasing a ball—to let you know the reading level of a book.

A

Learn to Read

Frequent repetition of sentence structures, high frequency words, and familiar topics provide ample support for brand new readers. Approximately 100 words.

1

Read Independently

Repetition is mixed with varied sentence structures and 6 to 8 content words per book are introduced with photo label and picture glossary supports. Approximately 150 words.

2

Read to Know More

These books feature a higher text load with additional nonfiction features such as more photos, time lines, and text divided into sections. Approximately 250 words.

Amicus Readers are published by **Amicus**
P.O. Box 1329, Mankato, Minnesota 56002
www.amicuspublishing.us

Printed in the United States of America at at Corporate
Graphics, in North Mankato, Minnesota.

Series Editor   Rebecca Glaser
Series Designer   Bobbi J. Wyss
Photo Researcher   Heather Dreisbach

Library of Congress Cataloging-in-Publication Data
Adamson, Heather, 1974-
 Surviving a flood / by Heather Adamson.
    p. cm. – (Amicus Readers. Be prepared)
 Includes index.
 Summary: "Discusses the dangers of floods, how to
prepare for them, and how to stay safe during and after
a flood"–Provided by publisher.
 ISBN 978-1-60753-150-0 (library binding)
 1. Floods–Juvenile literature. 2. Floods–Safety
measures–Juvenile literature. I. Title.
 GB1399.A33 2012
 613.6'9–dc22
                                    2010041759

Photo Credits

NOEL CELIS/AFP/Getty Images, Cover; Stock Connection Blue / Alamy, Title Page; GERARD JULIEN/AFP/
Getty Images, 5; Robert Cianflone/Getty Images, 7, 20bl; Mayumi Terao/iStockphoto, 8, 21mr1; Bobbi Wyss/
NOAA, 9, 21mr2; Scott Olson/Getty Images, 11, 21br; Stephen Morton/Getty Images, 12; Lisa F. Young/
Shutterstock, 13; m c photography / Alamy, 14, 20ml; TORSTEN BLACKWOOD/AFP/Getty Images, 15;
FEMA/Tim Burkitt, 17, 21tr; © GREG RYAN / Alamy, 19; youding xie/iStockphoto, 20tl; Coprid/Shutterstock,
22a; Iwona Grodzka/iStockphoto, 22b; Timmary/Shutterstock, 22c

1035   3-2011
10 9 8 7 6 5 4 3 2 1

Table of Contents

Floods

Floods can happen anywhere in the world. Heavy rain, melting snow, **earthquakes**, and storms all cause flooding. You can learn how to stay safe in a flood.

5

Fast, hard rains set off **flash floods**. Water quickly overruns streets and homes. There isn't much time to prepare. People must move to high ground fast.

6

flash flood

floodplain

Lowlands near rivers and lakes are called **floodplains**. Scientists track storm paths, rainfall, and how fast snow melts. Then they **forecast** where floods might go. They warn people living in floodplains of rising water.

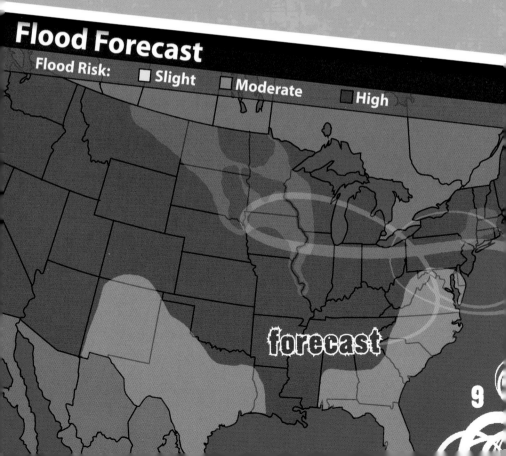

Flood Forecast

Flood Risk: ☐ Slight ☐ Moderate ☐ High

forecast

Preparing for a Flood

People try to control floodwaters. People fill bags with sand. They stack the sandbags around homes and buildings. They build large dirt walls called **levees**.

SPEED LIMIT 25

GENERATOR

levee

11

Even with levees and sandbags, floodwaters cannot always be stopped. You may be stuck without power or clean water for a few days.

Make a storm kit with food, water, and flashlights. Then you can wait for the water to go down or for help to arrive.

Sometimes people must **evacuate** in a flood. This means you must leave your home. Have a suitcase packed and a plan for where to stay. Don't forget to make plans for your pets.

15

After a Flood

Floods leave behind mud, germs, and mold. People get sick if buildings are not cleaned well.

Flood inspectors check buildings for water damage. Don't go back in a flooded building until everything is safe.

flood inspector

17

Floods are not fun. But they are part of how water moves on the earth. As long as there is water, people will have to deal with floods. You can stay safe if you are prepared.

Photo Glossary

earthquake
a sudden shaking of the earth that can cause cracks and other damage; earthquakes may cause floods.

evacuate
to leave an unsafe area; people evacuate to higher ground during floods.

flash flood
a flood that happens quickly without much time to prepare

flood inspector

someone who is trained to check buildings, gas lines, and power lines for safety after a flood

floodplain

a low area of ground near where waters run

forecast

to study weather and water patterns and guess where a storm or flood may hit

levee

a wall or dam to hold back water; many communities build dirt levees to hold back floodwaters.

21

Activity: Make a Flood

Try making this model to see how floods work.

What You Need:

Small, flat pan

Dirt or sand

Pitcher of water

1. Fill a small pan or flat container halfway with dirt or sand.

2. Slowly pour a little water in the pan. What happens?

3. Now pour the water faster. What happens? When the water comes slowly, it soaks into the dirt or sand. When the water comes too fast, it makes puddles. The same thing happens in a flood. Water comes faster than it can soak into the ground or run down the river.

Ideas for Parents and Teachers

Be Prepared, an Amicus Readers Level 2 series, provides simple explanations of what storms are and offers reassuring steps that kids and families can take to be prepared for disasters. As you read this book with your children or students, use the ideas below to help them get even more out of their reading experience.

Before Reading

* Read the title and ask the students if they've ever experienced a flood or know someone who has.

* Ask the students how they would know when there was a flood nearby. Ask them why we need to be prepared for floods.

* Use the photo glossary words to help them predict what they will learn from the book.

Read the Book

* Ask the students to read the book independently.

* Provide support where necessary. Point out that the photo labels can help them learn new words.

After Reading

* Ask the students to retell what they learned about floods and how to prepare for them. Compare their answers to what they said before reading the book.

* Have students do the activity on page 22 and talk about how much water the land can absorb.

Index

Web Sites

FEMA for Kids: Floods
http://www.fema.gov/kids/floods.htm

Flood Zone Kids: Introduction
http://www.floodfacts.com/floodzone_kids_intro.html

Weather Wiz Kids: Rain and Floods
http://www.weatherwizkids.com/weather-rain.htm